true
spirituality

Becoming a Romans 12 Christian

Table of Contents

How to Start Your Own Small Group

The fact that you are even reading this page says a lot about you. It says that you are either one of those people that has to read everything, or it says you are open to God using you to lead a group.

Leading a small group can sound intimidating, but it really doesn't have to be. Think of it more as gathering a few friends to get to know each other better and to have some discussion around spiritual matters.

Here are a few practical tips to help you get started:

1. **Pray** — One of the most important principles of spiritual leadership is to realize you can't do this on your own. No matter how long you've been a Christian or been involved in ministry, you need the power of the Holy Spirit. Lean on Him; He will help you.

2. **Invite some friends** — Don't be afraid to ask people to come to your group. You will be surprised how many people are open to a study like this. Whether you have 4 or 14 in your group, it can be a powerful experience. You should probably plan on at least an hour and a half for your group meeting.

3. **Get your materials** — You will need to get a DVD of the video teaching done by Chip Ingram or use the streaming code found in the front of the Study Guide. You can get the DVD from www.livingontheedge.org. Also, it will be helpful for each person to have their own study guide. You can also purchase those through the website.

4. **Be prepared to facilitate** — Just a few minutes a week in preparation can make a huge difference in the group experience. Each week, preview the video teaching and review the discussion questions. If you don't think your group can get through all the questions, select the ones that are most relevant to your group.

6. **Learn to say "I don't know"** — This *True Spirituality* series is going to explore the most essential components of being a follower of Jesus. These sessions will spark some lively and spirited discussions. When tough questions come up, it's ok for you to say, "I don't know." Take the pressure off. No one expects you to have all the answers.

7. **Love your group** — Maybe the most important thing you bring to the group is your personal care for them. If you will pray for them, encourage them, call them, email them, involve them, and love them, God will be pleased and you will have a lot of fun along the way.

Thank you for your availability. May God bless you as you serve Him by serving others.

How to Get the Most Out of This Experience

You are about to begin a powerful journey exploring Romans 12, the executive summary of what it means to be a disciple of Jesus. There is a lot of confusion among Christians and churches about what it means to live like a Christian. This powerful series, taught by Chip Ingram, will cut through the clutter and confusion. The teaching comes straight out of Scripture (Romans 12) and will present a clear and compelling picture of a true follower of Jesus.

Listed below are the segments you will experience each week as well as some hints for getting the most out of this experience. If you are leading the group, you will find some additional help and coaching on pages 105-118.

1. Take It In Watch the video

It is important for us to get before God and submit ourselves to his truth. During this section, you will watch the video teaching by Chip. He will introduce each session with a personal word to the group, followed by the teaching portion of the video. At the end of the teaching segment, Chip will wrap up the session and help the group dive into discussion.

A teaching outline with fill-ins is provided for each session. As you follow along, write down questions or insights that you can share during the discussion time.

Even though most of the verses will appear on the screen and in your notes, it is a great idea to bring your own Bible each week. It will allow you to make notes in your own Bible and find other passages that might be relevant to that week's study.

2. Talk It Over

We not only grow by listening to God's word, but we grow in community. The friendship and insights of those in the group will enrich your small group experience. Several discussion questions are provided for your group to further engage the teaching content. Keep the following guidelines in mind for having a healthy group discussion.

- **Be involved.** Jump in and share your thoughts. Your ideas are important, and you have a perspective that is unique and can benefit the other group members.

- **Be a good listener.** Value what others are sharing. Seek to really understand the perspectives of others in your group, and don't be afraid to ask follow-up questions.

- **Be courteous.** People hold strong opinions about the topics in this study. Spirited discussion is great; disrespect and attack is not. When there is disagreement, focus on the issue and never turn the discussion into a personal attack.

- **Be focused.** Stay on topic. Help the group explore the subject at hand, and try to save unrelated questions or stories for afterwards.

- **Be careful not to dominate.** Be aware of the amount of talking you are doing in proportion to the rest of the group, and make space for others to speak.

- **Be a learner.** Stay sensitive to what God might be wanting to teach you through the lesson, as well as through what others have to say. Focus more on your own growth rather than making a point or winning an argument.

3. Live It Out – B.I.O.

Bio is a word that is synonymous with "life." Found in those three simple letters — B.I.O. — is the key to helping you become the person God wants you to be.

B = COME "BEFORE GOD" DAILY

Meet with Him personally through prayer and His word to enjoy His presence, receive His direction, and follow His will.

I = DO LIFE "IN COMMUNITY" WEEKLY

Structure your week to personally connect in safe relationships that provide love, support, transparency, challenge, and accountability.

O = BE "ON MISSION" 24/7

Cultivate a mindset to live out Jesus' love for others through acts of sacrifice as well as service at home, work, play, and church.

4. Accelerate (20 minutes that turn concepts into convictions)

Inspiration comes from hearing God's Word. **Motivation** grows by discussing God's Word. **Transformation** occurs when you study it for yourself. If you want to "accelerate" your growth, here is an assignment you can do at home each week. Our convictions become even stronger when we dig into Scripture and discover truth for ourselves. To help you get the most out of this exercise, consider partnering with somebody in your group who will also commit to doing the assignment this week. Then, after you have each finished the assignment, agree to spend 10 minutes sharing what you learned and what you are applying.

session 1

God's Dream For Your Life

ALL PARENTS HAVE A DREAM

- Our kids can be the source of our greatest _Pain_ or deepest _joy_.

- Our Heavenly Father has a dream for every one of His children.

- God's dream is to make you like His _Son_.
  Matthew 5:48, Romans 8:29, Ephesians 4:13

- God's dream for every child of His is to become a disciple—
  a _Romans 12_ Christian.

- Romans 12 is the _executive summary_
  of what it means to be a disciple.

5 Key Relationships ▶ Romans 12 Biblical Response

Being a Romans 12 Christian is first and foremost _relational_.

Romans 12 Overview

- Relationship with God
- Relationship with the world
- Relationship with yourself
- Relationship with believers
- Relationship with nonbelievers

Being a Romans 12 Christian is also _practical & measurable_.

1. Relationship with God ▶ _surrender_ to God

> Therefore, I urge you, brothers, in view of God's mercy, to offer
> your bodies as living sacrifices, holy and pleasing to God—this is
> your spiritual act of worship.

ROMANS 12:1 (NIV)

This verse answers the question, "How do you give God what He wants the most?"

The missing ingredient = _power_.

2. Relationship with the World ▶ _separate_ from the World.

> Do not conform any longer to the pattern of this world, but be transformed by the renewing of your mind. Then you will be able to test and approve what God's will is—his good, pleasing and perfect will.

ROMANS 12:2 (NIV)

This verse answers the question, "How do you get the very best from God?"

The missing ingredient = _peace_.

Talk It Over

1. As you were growing up, what was your view of God? What was He like and how has that view changed?

   _____

   _____

   _____

2. In your opinion, why are so many Christians not living out the dream God has for them?

   _____

   _____

   _____

3. How has your view of a mature Christian (disciple) changed? Why?

_____

_____

_____

4. Chip said, "being a Romans 12 Christian is first and foremost relational." What are some other words that Christians might say are first and foremost in being a good Christian? For you personally, what are the implications of viewing the Christian life as relational?

_____

_____

_____

Live It Out – B.I.O.

Bio is a word that is synonymous with "life." Found in those three simple letters — B.I.O. — is the key to helping you become the person God wants you to be.

B = COME "BEFORE GOD" DAILY

Meet with Him personally through prayer and His word to enjoy His presence, receive His direction, and follow His will.

I = DO LIFE "IN COMMUNITY" WEEKLY

Structure your week to personally connect in safe relationships that provide love, support, transparency, challenge, and accountability.

O = BE "ON MISSION" 24/7

Cultivate a mindset to live out Jesus' love for others through acts of sacrifice as well as service at home, work, play, and church.

Come Before God

5. Becoming like Jesus requires you developing a personal, intimate relationship with your heavenly Father. What does that look like in your everyday life? And what is a step you need to take to go deeper in your relationship with God?

    _____

    _____

    _____

Do Life In Community

6. Chip said God's dream is to make you like His Son. Part of what God uses to make you like His Son is authentic relationships with others (biblical community). Who in your life has had significant impact on helping you become more like Jesus?

    _____

    _____

    _____

Be On Mission

7. "The greatest need today is for Christians to live like Christians." Describe what "living like a Christian" means for your life. Get specific and practical.

    _____

    _____

    _____

Accelerate (20 minutes that turns concepts into convictions)

Inspiration comes from hearing God's Word. **Motivation** grows by discussing God's Word. **Transformation** occurs when you study it for yourself. If you want to "accelerate" your growth, here is an assignment you can do at home each week. Our convictions become even stronger when we dig into Scripture and discover truth for ourselves. To help you get the most out of this exercise, consider partnering with somebody in your group who will also commit to doing the assignment this week. Then, after you have each finished the assignment, agree to spend 10 minutes sharing what you learned and what you are applying.

Come Before God

1. Read the following passage through a couple of times. Read it slowly, really paying attention to the flow of what Paul is saying.

    ¹Therefore, I urge you, brothers and sisters, in view of God's mercy, to offer your bodies as a living sacrifice, holy and pleasing to God—this is your true and proper worship. ²Do not conform to the pattern of this world, but be transformed by the renewing of your mind. Then you will be able to test and approve what God's will is—his good, pleasing and perfect will.

    ³For by the grace given me I say to every one of you: Do not think of yourself more highly than you ought, but rather think of yourself with sober judgment, in accordance with the faith God has distributed to each of you. ⁴For just as each of us has one body with many members, and these members do not all have the same function, ⁵so in Christ we, though many, form one body, and each member belongs to all the others. ⁶We have different gifts, according to the grace given to each of us. If your gift is prophesying, then prophesy in accordance with your faith; ⁷if it is serving, then serve; if it is teaching, then teach; ⁸if it is to encourage, then give encouragement; if it is giving, then give generously; if it is to lead, do it diligently; if it is to show mercy, do it cheerfully.

    ROMANS 12:1-8 (NIV)

2. Go through this passage and circle all of the commands. Look for verbs and action words.

3. Why do you think Paul uses the imagery of "living sacrifice" to describe surrender? What are some characteristics of a living sacrifice?

    _____

    _____

    _____

4. Spend a few minutes coming before God in prayer, asking Him to reveal anything that stands between you and total surrender.

Do Life In Community

5. In verse 5, Paul says, "...so in Christ we, though many, form one body, and each member belongs to all the others." Write out some specific characteristics of what it means to "belong to all the others."

    _____

    _____

    _____

Be On Mission

6. Read over Romans 12:2 again. How is being "separate from the world" crucial to being "on mission?" Is there some area where you have been conformed to the pattern of this world? What steps do you need to take to be separate from the world system?

session 2

God's Dream For Your Life
PART TWO

5 Key Relationships ▶ Romans 12 Biblical Responses

1. Relationship with God ▶ Surrender to God (covered in Session 1)

2. Relationship with the World ▶ Separate from the World (covered in Session 1)

3. Relationship with Yourself ▶ _____Sober_____ in Self-Assessment

> For by the grace given me I say to every one of you: Do not think of yourself more highly than you ought, but rather think of yourself with sober judgment, in accordance with the measure of faith God has given you. Just as each of us has one body with many members, and these members do not all have the same function, so in Christ we who are many form one body, and each member belongs to all the others. We have different gifts, according to the grace given us. If a man's gift is prophesying, let him use it in proportion to his faith. If it is serving, let him serve; if it is teaching, let him teach; if it is encouraging, let him encourage; if it is contributing to the needs of others, let him give generously; if it is leadership, let him govern diligently; if it is showing mercy, let him do it cheerfully.

ROMANS 12:3-8 (NIV)

These verses answer the question, "How do you come to grips with the real you?"

The missing ingredient = _____Purpose_____

4. Relationship with Believers ▶ _____Serving_____ in Love

> Love must be sincere. Hate what is evil; cling to what is good.
> Be devoted to one another in brotherly love. Honor one another
> above yourselves. Never be lacking in zeal, but keep your spiritual
> fervor, serving the Lord. Be joyful in hope, patient in affliction,
> faithful in prayer. Share with God's people who are in need.
> Practice hospitality.

ROMANS 12:9-13 (NIV)

These verses answer the question, "How do I experience authentic community?"

The missing ingredient = God's _____presence_____

5. Relationship with Nonbelievers ▶ _____supernaturally_____ Responding to Evil with Good

> Bless those who persecute you; bless and do not curse. Rejoice
> with those who rejoice; mourn with those who mourn. Live in
> harmony with one another. Do not be proud, but be willing to
> associate with people of low position. Do not be conceited. Do
> not repay anyone evil for evil. Be careful to do what is right in the
> eyes of everybody. If it is possible, as far as it depends on you,
> live at peace with everyone. Do not take revenge, my friends, but
> leave room for God's wrath, for it is written: 'It is mine to avenge;
> I will repay,' says the Lord. On the contrary: 'If your enemy is
> hungry, feed him; if he is thirsty, give him something to drink. In
> doing this, you will heap burning coals on his head.' Do not be
> overcome by evil, but overcome evil with good.

ROMANS 12:14-21 (NIV)

These verses answer the question, "How do you overcome the evil aimed at you?"

The missing ingredient = ___Perspective___

- Danger – Romans 12 is not a moral code to live up to, but a faith response to what God has already done for us.

    - Romans 1–3: Sin – Our problem that separates us from God.

    - Romans 4–5: Salvation – God's solution in the work of Jesus Christ on the cross.

    - Romans 6–8: Sanctification – Living your new life in God's power and growing progressively in Christ-likeness.

    - Romans 9–11: Sovereignty – Living in confidence because God is in control and keeps all His promises.

Talk It Over

1. When you were growing up, what did it mean to be a good Christian? Was it more grace oriented or more performance oriented?

    _____

    _____

    _____

2. Read Matthew 23:1-7, 25-28. From these verses, what evidence of "image management" can you find in the Pharisees?

    _____

    _____

    _____

3. Chip talked about the importance of a "sober self-assessment". What are some of the negative results of not having an accurate self-assessment?

    _____

    _____

    _____

Live It Out - B.I.O.

Bio is a word that is synonymous with "life." Found in those three simple letters — B.I.O. — is the key to helping you become the person God wants you to be.

B = COME "BEFORE GOD" DAILY

Meet with Him personally through prayer and His word to enjoy His presence, receive His direction, and follow His will.

I = DO LIFE "IN COMMUNITY" WEEKLY

Structure your week to personally connect in safe relationships that provide love, support, transparency, challenge, and accountability.

O = BE "ON MISSION" 24/7

Cultivate a mindset to live out Jesus' love for others through acts of sacrifice as well as service at home, work, play, and church.

Come Before God

4.   Read the following passage from Romans 8.

[14]For those who are led by the Spirit of God are the children of God. [15]The Spirit you received does not make you slaves, so that you live in fear again; rather, the Spirit you received brought about your adoption to sonship. And by him we cry, "Abba, Father." [16]The Spirit himself testifies with our spirit that we are God's children. [17]Now if we are children, then we are heirs—heirs of God and co-heirs with Christ, if indeed we share in his sufferings in order that we may also share in his glory.

ROMANS 8:14-17 (NIV)

As you think about having an accurate view of yourself, what does this passage teach us about our true identity in Christ? What phrase from this passage most connects with you? Why?

_____

_____

_____

Do Life In Community

5. As a group, brainstorm a list of the top five characteristics of authentic community. Which one of these characteristics do you think your group needs to work on?

_____

_____

_____

_____

_____

_____

6. When in your Christian life have you most experienced true community (authentic relationships)?

_____

_____

_____

Be On Mission

7. What phrase or verse most stands out to you from Romans 12:14–21? Why? In your life, in what practical ways can you "overcome evil with good"?

_____

_____

_____

Accelerate (20 minutes that turns concepts into convictions)

Inspiration comes from hearing God's Word. **Motivation** grows by discussing God's Word. **Transformation** occurs when you study it for yourself. If you want to "accelerate" your growth, here is an assignment you can do at home each week. Our convictions become even stronger when we dig into Scripture and discover truth for ourselves. To help you get the most out of this exercise, consider partnering with somebody in your group who will also commit to doing the assignment this week. Then, after you have each finished the assignment, agree to spend 10 minutes sharing what you learned and what you are applying.

Come Before God

1. Carefully and slowly read this passage over a couple of times. In order to focus and slow down, you might even try reading the passage out loud.

    [9]Love must be sincere. Hate what is evil; cling to what is good. [10]Be devoted to one another in love. Honor one another above yourselves. [11]Never be lacking in zeal, but keep your spiritual fervor, serving the Lord. [12]Be joyful in hope, patient in affliction, faithful in prayer. [13]Share with the Lord's people who are in need. Practice hospitality.

    [14]Bless those who persecute you; bless and do not curse. [15]Rejoice with those who rejoice; mourn with those who mourn. [16]Live in harmony with one another. Do not be proud, but be willing to associate with people of low position. Do not be conceited.

    [17]Do not repay anyone evil for evil. Be careful to do what is right in the eyes of everyone. [18]If it is possible, as far as it depends on you, live at peace with everyone. [19]Do not take revenge, my dear friends, but leave room for God's wrath, for it is written: "It is mine to avenge; I will repay," says the Lord. [20]On the contrary:

    "If your enemy is hungry, feed him; if he is thirsty, give him something to drink. In doing this, you will heap burning coals on his head."

    [21]Do not be overcome by evil, but overcome evil with good.

    ROMANS 12:9-21 (NIV)

2. Romans 12:9-13 gives us the principles of authentic community. Acts 2:42-47 shows us authentic community being lived out in the early church. Read Acts 2:42-47 and make a list of the characteristics of true community found in that passage.

    _____

    _____

    _____

3. In verse 9, Paul says that "love must be sincere". Literally that means that love doesn't wear a mask. When do you find yourself wearing a mask? What is the fear that causes you to wear a mask?

    _____

    _____

    _____

4. Compare Paul's teaching in Romans 12:14-21 with the story of the crucifixion in Luke 23. In what specific ways does Jesus embody the teaching of Romans 12:14-21?

    _____

    _____

    _____

Do Life In Community

5. From the following phrases out of Romans 12:9–13, put a check mark by the ones that you think you need to work on. Then, circle the one that you are willing to take a next step in.

☐ Love must be sincere

☐ Hate what is evil

☐ Be devoted to one another

☐ Honor one another above yourselves

☐ Faithful in prayer

☐ Share with the Lord's people in need

☐ Practice hospitality

As a follow-up, have a brief conversation with a friend this week about this passage and the next step you have committed to take.

Be On Mission

6. As you think about being "on mission", what one phrase or verse from Romans 12:14–21 can you put into practice this week?

session 3

How To Give God What He Wants The Most

Take It In Watch the video

Introduction – "Risk, Reason, and the Decision-Making Process"

Case Study #1 – John's Civil War Coins

Case Study #2 – Sheila's Picasso

- **Questions to Ponder**

    1. What are the risks?

    2. What are the potential rewards?

    3. What would you do?

    4. Why?

3 Principles for Making Big Decisions

1. In every big decision you need _truth_.

2. In every big decision you need _Knowledge_.

3. In every big decision you need _faith_.

Case Study #3 – Ancient Treasure

The kingdom of heaven is like a treasure hidden in the field, which a man found and hid again; and from joy over it he goes and sells all that he has and buys that field. Again, the kingdom of heaven is like a merchant looking for fine pearls. When he found one of great value, he went away and sold everything he had and bought it.

JESUS, MATTHEW 13:44–46 (NASB)

- **Observations**

    1. A man finds a treasure.

    2. He hides it again.

    3. He has an emotional response.

    4. He sells everything he has so he can get the treasure.

                        Surrender

- **Thesis** — Total commitment is the ___*channel*___
  through which God's biggest and best blessings flow.

- **Definition** — "Total commitment is the alignment of one's motives, resources, priorities, and goals to fulfill a specific mission, accomplish a specific task, or follow a specific person."

- **Spiritual Insight** — Through which lens do you view total commitment?

Positive	vs.	Negative
Wise		Sacrifice
Logical		Self-denial
Shrewd		Noble, martyr
Re-evaluation		Renunciation

Talk It Over

1. When you think of surrender or total commitment, do you see it through the lens negatively or positively? Why?

    ----

2. What is your biggest barrier to surrender? In the past, what was the number one fear that kept you from surrendering to Christ? Is there anything now that keeps you from surrendering?

_____

_____

_____

3. Chip said that "total commitment" is the channel through which God's best and biggest blessings flow. How have you experienced the truth of this statement?

_____

_____

_____

4. Who is the most committed Christian you know? What is it about their life that is different?

_____

_____

_____

Live It Out – B.I.O.

Bio is a word that is synonymous with "life." Found in those three simple letters — B.I.O. — is the key to helping you become the person God wants you to be.

B = COME "BEFORE GOD" DAILY

Meet with Him personally through prayer and His word to enjoy His presence, receive His direction, and follow His will.

I = DO LIFE "IN COMMUNITY" WEEKLY

Structure your week to personally connect in safe relationships that provide love, support, transparency, challenge, and accountability.

O = BE "ON MISSION" 24/7

Cultivate a mindset to live out Jesus' love for others through acts of sacrifice as well as service at home, work, play, and church.

Come Before God

5.   Romans 6:16–18 (NLT) says, "Don't you realize that you become the slave of whatever you choose to obey? You can be a slave to sin, which leads to death, or you can choose to obey God, which leads to righteous living. Thank God! Once you were slaves of sin, but now you wholeheartedly obey this teaching we have given you. Now you are free from your slavery to sin, and you have become slaves to righteous living."

What does this passage teach us about "surrender"?

_____

_____

_____

Do Life In Community

6.   One of the problems with a "living sacrifice" is that it can crawl off the altar. Share with the group your biggest challenge in staying "surrendered" (totally committed). Spend a little time praying for one another, asking God to help each of those in your group to be "all in."

_____

_____

_____

Be On Mission

7.   If you were "all in," how would your life be different this next month? How would it impact you being "on mission?"

_____

_____

_____

Accelerate (20 minutes that turns concepts into convictions)

Inspiration comes from hearing God's Word. **Motivation** grows by discussing God's Word. **Transformation** occurs when you study it for yourself. If you want to "accelerate" your growth, here is an assignment you can do at home each week. Our convictions become even stronger when we dig into Scripture and discover truth for ourselves. To help you get the most out of this exercise, consider partnering with somebody in your group who will also commit to doing the assignment this week. Then, after you have each finished the assignment, agree to spend 10 minutes sharing what you learned and what you are applying.

Come Before God

1. Carefully and slowly read the following passage a couple of times.

> ⁵I was circumcised when I was eight days old. I am a pure-blooded citizen of Israel and a member of the tribe of Benjamin—a real Hebrew if there ever was one! I was a member of the Pharisees, who demand the strictest obedience to the Jewish law. ⁶I was so zealous that I harshly persecuted the church. And as for righteousness, I obeyed the law without fault.
>
> ⁷I once thought these things were valuable, but now I consider them worthless because of what Christ has done. ⁸Yes, everything else is worthless when compared with the infinite value of knowing Christ Jesus my Lord. For his sake I have discarded everything else, counting it all as garbage, so that I could gain Christ ⁹and become one with him. I no longer count on my own righteousness through obeying the law; rather, I become righteous through faith in Christ. For God's way of making us right with himself depends on faith. ¹⁰I want to know Christ and experience the mighty power that raised him from the dead. I want to suffer with him, sharing in his death, ¹¹so that one way or another I will experience the resurrection from the dead!

PHILIPPIANS 3:5–11 (NLT)

2. In Philippians 3:5–6, what are some potential barriers that could have kept Paul from being "all in"?

_____

_____

_____

3. In Philippians 3:7–8, circle the words that reflect Paul's view of his past credentials.

_____

_____

_____

4. Write out a prayer of surrender. Set aside enough time to carefully consider your prayer. In your own words, let God know that you are "all in."

_____

_____

_____

Do Life In Community

5. Get together with a friend or someone in your small group and have a discussion about "surrender" (total commitment).

   Discuss the following questions:

   • What fears have kept you from total surrender?

   • How does your view of God impact surrender?

   • What are the practical implications of surrender in your life?

6. How does "surrender" impact your perspective on the purpose of your life? Is there a next step you need to take to be obedient to God's purpose for your life?

true
spirituality

Becoming a Romans 12 Christian

session 4

How To Give God What He Wants The Most
PART TWO

Take It In Watch the video

- **The Problem** = What does total commitment look like in our relationship with God? How does it work?

- **The Answer** = Romans 12:1

  Therefore, I urge you, brothers, in view of God's mercy, to offer your bodies as living sacrifices, holy and pleasing to God—this is your spiritual act of worship.

  ROMANS 12:1 (NIV)

- **The Command** = "___offer___ your bodies"
- **The Motivation** = "the ___mercy___ of God"
- **The Reason** = "spiritual act of ___worship___"
- What Does He Want Most?

  God wants ___you___!

Talk It Over

1. From your observation and experience, what are some fears that keep people from going all in?

   _____

   _____

   _____

2. Paul says that the motivation for our surrender is God's mercy. What does God's mercy have to do with surrender?

   _____

   _____

   _____

3. In what way is surrender to God like the commitment of marriage?

    _____

    _____

    _____

4. Read the following prayer out loud to the group. What part of this prayer most resonates with you? Why?

    _____

    _____

    _____

God, be Thou exalted over my possessions.

Nothing of earth's treasures shall seem dear unto me if only Thou are glorified in my life. Be Thou exalted over my friendships. I am determined that Thou shalt be above all, though I must stand deserted and alone in the midst of the earth. Be Thou exalted above my comforts. Though it mean the loss of bodily comforts and the carrying of heavy crosses, I shall keep my vow made this day before Thee. Be Thou exalted over my reputation. Make me ambitious to please Thee even if as a result I must sink into obscurity and my name be forgotten as a dream. Rise, O Lord, into Thy proper place of honor, above my ambitions, above my likes and dislikes, above my family, my health and even my life itself. Let me sink that Thou mayest rise above.

A.W. TOZER

Live It Out – B.I.O.

Bio is a word that is synonymous with "life." Found in those three simple letters — B.I.O. — is the key to helping you become the person God wants you to be.

B = COME "BEFORE GOD" DAILY

Meet with Him personally through prayer and His word to enjoy His presence, receive His direction, and follow His will.

I = DO LIFE "IN COMMUNITY" WEEKLY

Structure your week to personally connect in safe relationships that provide love, support, transparency, challenge, and accountability.

O = BE "ON MISSION" 24/7

Cultivate a mindset to live out Jesus' love for others through acts of sacrifice as well as service at home, work, play, and church.

Come Before God

5.   Psalm 84:11 says:

> For the LORD God is a sun and shield; the LORD bestows favor and honor; no good thing does he withhold from those whose walk is blameless.

PSALM 84:11 (NIV)

What are some insights from this verse that help us in our journey to surrender?

Do Life In Community

6. We have to constantly renew our surrender to God. How can the people in your group help you in your journey to live a life of total surrender?

_____

_____

_____

Be On Mission

7. How will our relationships with unbelievers change if we are surrendered to God?

_____

_____

_____

Accelerate (20 minutes that turns concepts into convictions)

Inspiration comes from hearing God's Word. **Motivation** grows by discussing God's Word. **Transformation** occurs when you study it for yourself. If you want to "accelerate" your growth, here is an assignment you can do at home each week. Our convictions become even stronger when we dig into Scripture and discover truth for ourselves. To help you get the most out of this exercise, consider partnering up with somebody in your group who will also commit to doing the assignment this week. Then, after you have each finished the assignment, agree to spend 10 minutes sharing what you learned and what you are applying.

Come Before God

1. Read the story of Abraham and Isaac in Genesis 22:1–18.

2. Try to place yourself in Abraham's sandals. What would you have been feeling on that long walk to Mt. Moriah? What kinds of questions would you have had for God?

_____

_____

_____

3. According to Hebrews 11:17–19, what did Abraham believe would happen if he sacrificed his son Isaac?

_____

_____

_____

4. Is there anything that has become an idol (plastic beads) that stands in between you and God?

_____

_____

_____

Do Life In Community

5. Who do you need to ask to help you in your journey with total surrender? Get together with a friend and ask them for their help and then spend some time praying together.

_____

_____

_____

Be On Mission

6. Just like with Abraham, God has a long history of inviting his followers into a life of adventure. And it always requires us to move beyond our comfort zone. It is your confidence in the God you KNOW that gives confidence to step into the UNKNOWN.

    Is there anything that God is calling you to do that will require you to surrender? Spend some time praying and reflecting on that question. Then, obey whatever God reveals to you.

    _____

    _____

    _____

session 5

How To Get God's Best For Your Life

Why are there so many decisions and so few disciples?

- **Negative Command** — "Do not be conformed to the pattern of this world, but be transformed by the renewing of your mind. Then you will be able to test and approve what God's will is—his good, pleasing and perfect will" Romans 12:2 (NIV)

"Do not be conformed"

- Passive voice = the subject is being acted upon

- Imperative = a command

- Present tense = it is continuous

Translation — Stop allowing yourselves to be molded by the *influence* and *pressures* of this present world system.

Application — We are to be ___separate___ from the world's values.

Do not love the world nor the things in the world. If anyone loves the world, the love of the Father is not in him. For all that is in the world, the lust of the flesh and the lust of the eyes and the boastful pride of life, is not from the Father, but is from the world. The world is passing away, and also its lusts; but the one who does the will of God lives forever.

1 JOHN 2:15-17 (NASB)

- Lust of the flesh = passion to ___feel___ (pleasure)
- Lust of the eyes = passion to ___have___ (possessions)
- Pride of life = passion to ___be___ (position)

Summary - The world's system seeks to seduce us from our love for Christ by pleasure, possessions, and position.

- **Positive Command** - "...but be transformed by the renewing of your mind."

"Be transformed"

  - Passive voice = the subject is being acted upon

  - Imperative = a command

  - Present tense = it is continuous

Translation — Allow God to completely change your inward thinking and outward behavior by cooperating wholeheartedly moment-by-moment with the Spirit's renewing process.

Application — Are you shaped more by the world or the _____Word_____?

But He answered and said, "It is written, 'Man shall not live on bread alone, but on every word that proceeds out of the mouth of God.'"

MATTHEW 4:4 (NASB)

But we all, with unveiled face, beholding as in a mirror the glory of the Lord, are being transformed into the same image from glory to glory, just as from the Lord, the Spirit.

2 CORINTHIANS 3:18 (NASB)

Talk It Over

1. Where do you battle the most? What about the world's system draws you and tempts you the most?

    _____

    _____

    _____

2. What are some prominent values in our generation that are contrary to God's values?

    _____

    _____

    _____

3. Read John 17:13-18. What does it mean to be "in" the world, but not "of" the world?

    _____

    _____

    _____

4. As you think about your spiritual journey over the last couple of years, where has God been at work in transforming you?

    _____

    _____

    _____

Live It Out – B.I.O.

Bio is a word that is synonymous with "life." Found in those three simple letters — B.I.O. — is the key to helping you become the person God wants you to be.

B = COME "BEFORE GOD" DAILY

Meet with Him personally through prayer and His word to enjoy His presence, receive His direction, and follow His will.

I = DO LIFE "IN COMMUNITY" WEEKLY

Structure your week to personally connect in safe relationships that provide love, support, transparency, challenge, and accountability.

O = BE "ON MISSION" 24/7

Cultivate a mindset to live out Jesus' love for others through acts of sacrifice as well as service at home, work, play, and church.

Come Before God

5. When Jesus was tempted by Satan, He said, "It is written, 'Man shall not live on bread alone, but on every word that proceeds out of the mouth of God.'" Matthew 4:4 (NASB)

    What do you need to do to better prepare yourself for winning the battle of temptation?

    _____

    _____

    _____

Do Life In Community

6. We are constantly bombarded by the world's system. What can you do to support and help one another in the battle to be separate from the world?

    _____

    _____

    _____

Be On Mission

7. How can we protect our families from being infected by the world's system? Get practical and specific.

    _____

    _____

    _____

Accelerate (20 minutes that turns concepts into convictions)

Inspiration comes from hearing God's Word. **Motivation** grows by discussing God's Word. **Transformation** occurs when you study it for yourself. If you want to "accelerate" your growth, here is an assignment you can do at home each week. Our convictions become even stronger when we dig into Scripture and discover truth for ourselves. To help you get the most out of this exercise, consider partnering with somebody in your group who will also commit to doing the assignment this week. Then, after you have each finished the assignment, agree to spend 10 minutes sharing what you learned and what you are applying.

Come Before God

1. Read James 4:4–10 carefully and slowly.

⁴You adulterers! Don't you realize that friendship with the world makes you an enemy of God? I say it again: If you want to be a friend of the world, you make yourself an enemy of God. ⁵What do you think the Scriptures mean when they say that the spirit God has placed within us is filled with envy? ⁶But he gives us even more grace to stand against such evil desires. As the Scriptures say,

"God opposes the proud but favors the humble."

⁷So humble yourselves before God. Resist the devil, and he will flee from you. ⁸Come close to God, and God will come close to you. Wash your hands, you sinners; purify your hearts, for your loyalty is divided between God and the world. ⁹Let there be tears for what you have done. Let there be sorrow and deep grief. Let there be sadness instead of laughter, and gloom instead of joy. ¹⁰Humble yourselves before the Lord, and he will lift you up in honor.

JAMES 4:4–10 (NLT)

2.   Go through the passage and circle all of the actions we can take to remain separate from the world.

3.   In verse 4, why do you think God uses such strong language to talk about "friendship with the world"?

_____

_____

_____

4.   What do you sense God might be saying to you from this passage?

_____

_____

_____

Do Life In Community

5.   Have a discussion with your family or a good friend about this week's topic. Spend some time talking about the impact of media on our lives and how we should respond as Christ followers.

Be On Mission

6.   Is there some area where you have been compromising or hurting your testimony with unbelievers? In the words of James 4, has your loyalty been divided between God and the world? Spend some time praying and reflecting on these questions. Then, respond obediently to whatever God reveals to you.

_____

_____

_____

session 6

How To Get God's Best For Your Life

Take It In Watch the video

The Means of Transformation — "...by the renewing of your mind."

- Renewing your mind is a continual _refocus_ of a Romans 12:1 perspective. –Colossians 3:1–4

- Renewing your mind will always involve a _battle_. –2 Corinthians 10:4–5

- Renewing your mind is a _supernatural_ work of the Spirit. –Romans 8:5–6

Summary — You are what you _eat_!

Practical Methods for "Renewing Your Mind"

1. _Hearing_ God's Word – Romans 10:17 (NASB)

   "So faith comes from hearing, and hearing by the word of Christ."

2. _Reading_ God's Word – Revelation 1:3 (NASB)

   "Blessed is he who reads and those who hear the words of the prophecy, and heed the things which are written in it; for the time is near."

3. _Studying_ God's Word – 2 Timothy 2:15 (NASB)

   "Be diligent to present yourself approved to God as a workman who does not need to be ashamed, accurately handling the word of truth."

4. _Memorizing_ God's Word – Psalm 119:9, 11 (NASB)

"⁹How can a young man keep his way pure? By keeping it according to Your word."

"¹¹Your word I have treasured in my heart, that I may not sin against You."

5. _Meditating_ on God's Word – Joshua 1:8 (NASB)

"Do not let this Book of the Law depart from your mouth; meditate on it day and night, so that you may be careful to do everything written in it. Then you will be prosperous and successful."

Talk It Over

1. What one baby step do you need to take to renew your mind? And of those five things that we talked about, which one of those is lacking or do you need to take a baby step and address?

2. What specific practices have been most helpful in renewing your mind?

3. Psalm 19:8 (NLT) says, "The commandments of the LORD are right, bringing joy to the heart. The commands of the LORD are clear, giving insight to life." Share a personal example of how the word of God has given you insight into some life situation.

4. What is the biggest hindrance to you spending time in God's word on a regular basis?

_____

_____

_____

Live It Out – B.I.O.

Bio is a word that is synonymous with "life." Found in those three simple letters — B.I.O. — is the key to helping you become the person God wants you to be.

B = COME "BEFORE GOD" DAILY

Meet with Him personally through prayer and His word to enjoy His presence, receive His direction, and follow His will.

I = DO LIFE "IN COMMUNITY" WEEKLY

Structure your week to personally connect in safe relationships that provide love, support, transparency, challenge, and accountability.

O = BE "ON MISSION" 24/7

Cultivate a mindset to live out Jesus' love for others through acts of sacrifice as well as service at home, work, play, and church.

Come Before God

5. Read the following passage to the group:

[7]Be strong and very courageous. Be careful to obey all the law my servant Moses gave you; do not turn from it to the right or to the left, that you may be successful wherever you go. [8]Keep this Book of the Law always on your lips; meditate on it day and night, so that you may be careful to do everything written

in it. Then you will be prosperous and successful. ⁹Have I not commanded you? Be strong and courageous. Do not be afraid; do not be discouraged, for the LORD your God will be with you wherever you go.

JOSHUA 1:7-9 (NIV)

As you think about renewing your mind, what most stands out to you from this passage? What principles and practices do you see in this passage that are helpful when it comes to renewing your mind?

_____

_____

_____

Do Life In Community

6.   Share a verse or passage of Scripture that is especially meaningful to you and why this Scripture has special significance in your life.

_____

_____

_____

Be On Mission

7.   How does renewing our mind help us be "on mission"?

_____

_____

_____

Accelerate (20 minutes that turns concepts into convictions)

Inspiration comes from hearing God's Word. **Motivation** grows by discussing God's Word. **Transformation** occurs when you study it for yourself. If you want to "accelerate" your growth, here is an assignment you can do at home each week. Our convictions become even stronger when we dig into Scripture and discover truth for ourselves. To help you get the most out of this exercise, consider partnering with somebody in your group who will also commit to doing the assignment this week. Then, after you have each finished the assignment, agree to spend 10 minutes sharing what you learned and what you are applying.

Come Before God

1. Read these two excerpts from Psalm 119. Read them over a couple of times.

^{9}How can a young person stay on the path of purity? By living according to your word. ^{10}I seek you with all my heart; do not let me stray from your commands. ^{11}I have hidden your word in my heart that I might not sin against you. ^{12}Praise be to you, LORD; teach me your decrees. ^{13}With my lips I recount all the laws that come from your mouth. ^{14}I rejoice in following your statutes as one rejoices in great riches. ^{15}I meditate on your precepts and consider your ways. ^{16}I delight in your decrees; I will not neglect your word.

PSALM 119:9–16 (NIV)

^{33}Teach me, LORD, the way of your decrees, that I may follow it to the end. ^{34}Give me understanding, so that I may keep your law and obey it with all my heart. ^{35}Direct me in the path of your commands, for there I find delight. ^{36}Turn my heart toward your statutes and not toward selfish gain. ^{37}Turn my eyes away from worthless things; preserve my life according to your word. ^{38}Fulfill your promise to your servant, so that you may be feared. ^{39}Take away the disgrace I dread, for your laws are good. ⁴⁰How I long

for your precepts! In your righteousness preserve my life.

PSALM 119:33-40 (NIV)

2. Go through these passages and circle all of the ways and methods that we can engage the Word of God.

3. Now, go back through the passages and underline all of the words or phrases that describe the benefit of God's Word in our lives.

4. From these passages in Psalm 119, what do you sense God is asking you to do?

_____

_____

_____

Do Life In Community

6. In the video teaching from this session, Chip shared a practice that has been helpful in him renewing his mind. On some 3x5 cards, he wrote out something that he would like to see change in his life. He shared examples of being more authentic, dealing with people pleasing, and overcoming his workaholic tendencies. Then, he memorized a verse that addressed that issue in his life.

    Take the challenge of doing the same thing in your life. Write down on 3x5 cards three things you would like to see God change or renew in your life. Then, find a verse or two for each of those areas, and begin to review those cards daily and work on memorizing those verses. Finally, share with a good friend what you are working on and the verses you are trying to memorize. Ask for their help and accountability as you seek to let God renew your mind.

Be On Mission

7. Find a verse that connects to what you sense God has uniquely gifted and called you to do in serving him. Then, meditate on that verse, and commit it to memory in the new few weeks.

session 7

How To Come To Grips With The Real You

- **3 Questions We All Ask Ourselves:**

  1. Who am I? (Identity)

  2. Where do I belong? (Security)

  3. What am I supposed to do? (Significance)

- **Why is it so hard to answer these questions?**

[8]They heard the sound of the LORD God walking in the garden in the cool of the day, and the man and his wife hid themselves from the presence of the LORD God among the trees of the garden. [9]Then the LORD God called to the man, and said to him, "Where are you?" [10]He said, "I heard the sound of You in the garden, and I was afraid because I was naked, so I hid myself." [11]And He said, "Who told you that you were naked? Have you eaten from the tree of which I commanded you not to eat?" [12]The man said, "The woman whom You gave to be with me, she gave me from the tree, and I ate." [13]Then the LORD God said to the woman, "What is this you have done?" And the woman said, "The serpent deceived me, and I ate."

GENESIS 3:8-13 (NASB)

- **3 Obstacles to Getting Right Answers**

  1. Fear rooted in _Shame_.
     We learn to create personality holograms.

  2. Hiding rooted in _insecurity_.
     Everyone is desperately insecure.

  3. Blaming rooted in _denial_.

Talk It Over

1. What messages have you heard from your parents that shaped your view of yourself? What messages got down inside your soul and made you think, "This is who I am; this is what I'm like"?

    _____

    _____

    _____

2. Which of the three questions do you struggle with most? Explain.

    •   Who am I? (Identity)

    •   Where do I belong? (Security)

    •   What am I supposed to do? (Significance)

    _____

    _____

    _____

3. As a group, brainstorm a list of statements that are true about your identity in Christ. To get started, look at Romans 8 and Ephesians 1:3–14.

4. When in your life did you have the greatest sense of belonging?

    _____

    _____

    _____

5. Spend some time affirming one another. As you think about others in your group, complete the following statement: "One of the things I appreciate most about you is..."

Live It Out – B.I.O.

Bio is a word that is synonymous with "life." Found in those three simple letters — B.I.O. — is the key to helping you become the person God wants you to be.

B = COME "BEFORE GOD" DAILY

Meet with Him personally through prayer and His word to enjoy His presence, receive His direction, and follow His will.

I = DO LIFE "IN COMMUNITY" WEEKLY

Structure your week to personally connect in safe relationships that provide love, support, transparency, challenge, and accountability.

O = BE "ON MISSION" 24/7

Cultivate a mindset to live out Jesus' love for others through acts of sacrifice as well as service at home, work, play, and church.

Come Before God

6. Read Psalm 139:1–6 out loud to the group. What stands out to you most from this passage? Why?

Do Life In Community

7. Chip said that all of us are desperately insecure and we all create "personality holograms." What can you do to make your group the kind of place where people feel safe to take off their masks? Be specific.

Be On Mission

8. What are some practical strategies you can use to make sure your kids have a proper sense of identity?

_____

_____

_____

Accelerate (20 minutes that turns concepts into convictions)

Inspiration comes from hearing God's Word. **Motivation** grows by discussing God's Word. **Transformation** occurs when you study it for yourself. If you want to "accelerate" your growth, here is an assignment you can do at home each week. Our convictions become even stronger when we dig into Scripture and discover truth for ourselves. To help you get the most out of this exercise, consider partnering with somebody in your group who will also commit to doing the assignment this week. Then, after you have each finished the assignment, agree to spend 10 minutes sharing what you learned and what you are applying.

Come Before God

1. Read this passage in Ephesians 1 carefully and slowly.

³Praise be to the God and Father of our Lord Jesus Christ, who has blessed us in the heavenly realms with every spiritual blessing in Christ. ⁴For he chose us in him before the creation of the world to be holy and blameless in his sight. In love ⁵he predestined us for adoption to sonship through Jesus Christ, in accordance with his pleasure and will—⁶to the praise of his glorious grace, which he has freely given us in the One he loves. ⁷In him we have redemption through his blood, the forgiveness of sins, in accordance with the riches of God's grace ⁸that he lavished on us. With all wisdom and understanding, ⁹he made known to us the mystery of his will according to his good pleasure, which he

purposed in Christ, [10]to be put into effect when the times reach their fulfillment—to bring unity to all things in heaven and on earth under Christ.

[11]In him we were also chosen, having been predestined according to the plan of him who works out everything in conformity with the purpose of his will, [12]in order that we, who were the first to put our hope in Christ, might be for the praise of his glory. [13]And you also were included in Christ when you heard the message of truth, the gospel of your salvation. When you believed, you were marked in him with a seal, the promised Holy Spirit, [14]who is a deposit guaranteeing our inheritance until the redemption of those who are God's possession—to the praise of his glory.

EPHESIANS 1:3-14 (NIV)

2. Go through this passage and circle every spiritual blessing we have in Christ.

3. Now, go back through the passage and underline every place where you see God's name or a pronoun referring to God. Our identity is firmly anchored in HIS good work.

4. What do you sense God is wanting to say to you through this passage?

Do Life In Community

5. Take the challenge this week of writing a letter or email of blessing to someone you know. Remind them of who they are in Christ. You might even share some of these verses in Ephesians 1 as a reminder of what God thinks of them.

Be On Mission

7.   Ephesians 2:10 (NLT) says,

"For we are God's masterpiece. He has created us anew in Christ Jesus, so that we can do the good things he planned for us long ago."

When you are secure in the fact that you are indeed God's "masterpiece," you can stop focusing on yourself and start focusing on others.

Make it your mission this week to help people know how wonderfully created they are. Look for opportunities all week long to say to people, "I'm really glad God made you just the way He did. You're a gift to me." If you are a parent, make it a special point to do this with your kids.

session 8

How To Come To Grips With The Real You

- **God's Answers** - Romans 12:3-8 (NIV)

  1. Who are you? (v.3)

"For by the grace given me I say to every one of you: Do not think of yourself more highly than you ought, but rather think of yourself with sober judgment, in accordance with the measure of faith God has given you."

  The Command = Think _____ about yourself.

  2. Where do you belong? (v.4-5)

"Just as each of us has one body with many members, and these members do not all have the same function, so in Christ we who are many form one body, and each member belongs to all the others."

  The Reason = You have a _____ to fulfill.

3.   What are you supposed to do? (v.6-8)

"We have different gifts, according to the grace given us. If a man's gift is prophesying, let him use it in proportion to his faith. If it is serving, let him serve; if it is teaching, let him teach; if it is encouraging, let him encourage; if it is contributing to the needs of others, let him give generously; if it is leadership, let him govern diligently; if it is showing mercy, let him do it cheerfully."

The Practice = Discover and _____ your spiritual gift.

Never Forget Who You Really Are

1.   God uniquely created you—You are eternally _____.
(Psalm 139:13-14)

2.   God placed you in His family—You are unconditionally _____. (Ephesians 3:19-22)

3.   God gifted you to fulfill His purpose—You are irreplaceably _____. (Ephesians 2:10)

Talk It Over

1.   What are your three strengths and your three weaknesses?

_____

_____

_____

2. What is the most significant thing you have learned about yourself in the last 5 years?

_____

_____

_____

3. What is your primary spiritual gift? Where do you love to serve? Where do you feel effective and fulfilled when you serve?

_____

_____

_____

Do you feel like you are fully using your spiritual gift? If not, what is standing in the way?

_____

_____

_____

4. If time and money were not an issue, what would you attempt for God?

_____

_____

_____

Live It Out – B.I.O.

Bio is a word that is synonymous with "life." Found in those three simple letters — B.I.O. — is the key to helping you become the person God wants you to be.

B = COME "BEFORE GOD" DAILY

Meet with Him personally through prayer and His word to enjoy His presence, receive His direction, and follow His will.

I = DO LIFE "IN COMMUNITY" WEEKLY

Structure your week to personally connect in safe relationships that provide love, support, transparency, challenge, and accountability.

O = BE "ON MISSION" 24/7

Cultivate a mindset to live out Jesus' love for others through acts of sacrifice as well as service at home, work, play, and church.

Come Before God

5.   In Romans 12:4–5 (NIV) Paul says, "Just as each of us has one body with many members, and these members do not all have the same function, so in Christ we who are many form one body, and each member belongs to all the others."

What does it mean for each member to belong to all the others?

_____

_____

_____

Do Life In Community

6.   Ephesians 4:16 (NIV) says, "From him the whole body, joined and held together by every supporting ligament, grows and builds itself up in love, as each part does its work."

Spend a few minutes sharing how you see other people in the group. What are they good at? How do you see them contributing? Where do you see them fitting in the body of Christ?

_____

_____

_____

Be On Mission

7. As a group, brainstorm a project that would use the collective gifts of your group to serve and bless someone.

Accelerate (20 minutes that turns concepts into convictions)

Inspiration comes from hearing God's Word. **Motivation** grows by discussing God's Word. **Transformation** occurs when you study it for yourself. If you want to "accelerate" your growth, here is an assignment you can do at home each week. Our convictions become even stronger when we dig into Scripture and discover truth for ourselves. To help you get the most out of this exercise, consider partnering with somebody in your group who will also commit to doing the assignment this week. Then, after you have each finished the assignment, agree to spend 10 minutes sharing what you learned and what you are applying.

Come Before God

1. Read this passage from 1 Corinthians 12 carefully and slowly.

> [12] Just as a body, though one, has many parts, but all its many parts form one body, so it is with Christ. [13] For we were all baptized by one Spirit so as to form one body—whether Jews or Gentiles, slave or free—and we were all given the one Spirit to drink. [14] Even so the body is not made up of one part but of many.
>
> [15] Now if the foot should say, "Because I am not a hand, I do not belong to the body," it would not for that reason stop being part of the body. [16] And if the ear should say, "Because I am not an eye, I do not belong to the body," it would not for that reason stop being part of the body. [17] If the whole body were an eye, where would the sense of hearing be? If the whole body were an ear, where would the sense of smell be? [18] But in fact God has placed the parts in the body, every one of them, just as he wanted them

to be. ¹⁹If they were all one part, where would the body be? ²⁰As it is, there are many parts, but one body.

²¹The eye cannot say to the hand, "I don't need you!" And the head cannot say to the feet, "I don't need you!" ²²On the contrary, those parts of the body that seem to be weaker are indispensable, ²³and the parts that we think are less honorable we treat with special honor. And the parts that are unpresentable are treated with special modesty, ²⁴while our presentable parts need no special treatment. But God has put the body together, giving greater honor to the parts that lacked it, ²⁵so that there should be no division in the body, but that its parts should have equal concern for each other. ²⁶If one part suffers, every part suffers with it; if one part is honored, every part rejoices with it.

1 CORINTHIANS 12:12–26 (NIV)

2. What does this passage teach about issues of feeling inferior?
    (See verses 15–20)

    _____

    _____

    _____

3. What does this passage teach about issues of feeling superior?
    (See verses 21–26)

    _____

    _____

    _____

4. If you could summarize the three most important truths from this passage, what would they be?

    •

    •

    •

Do Life In Community

5. If you are struggling to know where you are gifted, try this exercise. Do an informal survey of people that know you well. Ask them this simple question: "Based on what I'm good at and passionate about, how could you see God using me to serve others?"

    _____

    _____

    _____

    The answer to that question will tell you a lot about how God has gifted you.

Be On Mission

6. The point of Paul's teaching on gifts in Romans 12:6-8 is that whatever gift we have been given by God, we should use it. Gifts are not toys to be played with or weapons to fight with; they are tools to build with.

    This week, what practical step will you take to use the gifts God has given you?

    _____

    _____

    _____

session 9

How To Experience Authentic Community

Take It In Watch the video

Why do so many good and sincere Christians get "spiritually stuck"?

Axiom — The greatest seed in the greatest soil cannot grow in the wrong
environment.

- The _Command_ of Jesus requires a very specific spiritual environment. (John 13:34-35)

- The _example_ of Jesus' ministry to develop His disciples demands a specific environment. (Mark 3:13-14)

- The _Practice_ of the early church and its impact argue for a specific environment. (Acts 2:42-47)

- The _history_ of the church past and present confirm a specific environment for spiritual growth and transformation.

The Spiritual Environment = _Authentic Community_

- The form this system takes is small groups.

- A Critical Distinction: Small Groups ≠ Authentic Community

The Principle - We must be engaged in the spiritual environment of authentic community for spiritual maturity to occur.

The 2 Big Questions

1. What is authentic community?

_____

_____

_____

2. How do you get it?

_____

_____

_____

Authentic Community Occurs When...

> [9]Let love be without hypocrisy. Abhor what is evil; cling to what is good. [10]Be devoted to one another in brotherly love; give preference to one another in honor; [11]not lagging behind in diligence, fervent in spirit, serving the Lord; [12]rejoicing in hope, persevering in tribulation, devoted to prayer, [13]contributing to the needs of the saints, practicing hospitality.

ROMANS 12:9-13 (NASB)

The real you... (v. 9)

meets real needs... (v. 10)

for the right reasons... (v. 11)

in the right way. (vs. 12-13)

The Real You Not a ___projection___ of yourself. (v. 9)
w/o hipocrisy

- Authenticity – "Let love be sincere."

- Purity – "Hate what is evil. Cling to what is good."

  Acts 5

Meets Real Needs Not convenient or ___Superficial___ ones. (v. 10)

- Devotion – "Be devoted to one another in brotherly love."

Talk It Over

1. Take what's going on in the life of this small group and line it up with Romans 12:9-13. Where do you need to take a baby step to move from being a good small group to having great community?

   _____

   _____

   _____

2. What can you do as a group to create the kind of safe environment where people in the group can truly be themselves and take off their masks? On the flip side, what things make the group feel unsafe?

    _____

    _____

    _____

3. Share a time when you needed the support of your friends to make it through a difficult time.

4. One of the characteristics of true community is that we "hate evil" and "cling to what is good." What does it look like practically for you to hate evil?

    _____

    _____

    _____

Live It Out – B.I.O.

Bio is a word that is synonymous with "life." Found in those three simple letters — B.I.O. — is the key to helping you become the person God wants you to be.

B = COME "BEFORE GOD" DAILY

Meet with Him personally through prayer and His word to enjoy His presence, receive His direction, and follow His will.

I = DO LIFE "IN COMMUNITY WEEKLY

Structure your week to personally connect in safe relationships that provide love, support, transparency, challenge, and accountability.

O = BE "ON MISSION" 24/7

Cultivate a mindset to live out Jesus' love for others through acts of sacrifice as well as service at home, work, play, and church.

Come Before God

5. Hebrews 10:24–25 (NIV) says, "And let us consider how we may spur one another on toward love and good deeds, not giving up meeting together, as some are in the habit of doing, but encouraging one another—and all the more as you see the Day approaching."

    What stands out to you from these verses? What insights from this passage can help you experience authentic community?

    _____

    _____

    _____

Do Life In Community

6. What would it take for your group to go to a deeper level of authentic community? What quality from Romans 12:9–13 would you like to see your group focus on?

    _____

    _____

    _____

Be On Mission

7. What is one need that you know of, inside or outside the group, that you could personally meet?

    _____

    _____

    _____

Accelerate (20 minutes that turns concepts into convictions)

Inspiration comes from hearing God's Word. **Motivation** grows by discussing God's Word. **Transformation** occurs when you study it for yourself. If you want to "accelerate" your growth, here is an assignment you can do at home each week. Our convictions become even stronger when we dig into Scripture and discover truth for ourselves. To help you get the most out of this exercise, consider partnering with somebody in your group who will also commit to doing the assignment this week. Then, after you have each finished the assignment, agree to spend 10 minutes sharing what you learned and what you are applying.

Come Before God

1. Carefully read the story of David and Jonathan's friendship in 1 Samuel 18:3-4; 19:4-5; 20:1-42.

2. 1 Samuel 18:3 says that David and Jonathan made a "covenant" with each other. In today's world, what would it look like to make a covenant of friendship with someone?

3. As you go through these passages, underline any action that demonstrates true and sacrificial friendship between these two men.

4. Make a list of the qualities of great friendship (community) that those actions represent.

   •

   •

   •

   •

Do Life In Community

5. This week, write a letter to someone who has provided true, authentic community in your life. Tell them what their friendship has meant to you and how their life has impacted you.

Be On Mission

6. Think of a person you'd like to get to know a little bit better. Take the initiative to get together with them.

session 10

How To Experience Authentic Community

Meets Real Need ▶ Not convenient or superficial ones. (v. 10)

- Devotion — "Be devoted to one another in brotherly love."

- Humility — "Giving preference to one another in honor."

> Do nothing from selfishness or empty conceit, but with humility of mind regard one another as more important than yourselves; do not merely look out for your own personal interests, but also for the interests of others.
>
> **PHILIPPIANS 2:3–4 (NASB)**

For the Right Reason ▶ Not to _____ people. (v. 11)

- Motive – "Not lagging behind in diligence, fervent in spirit, serving the Lord."

- Method – Genuine service to God is characterized by:

  - Diligence: Doing what God calls you to do when God calls you to do it.

  - Enthusiasm: Passion

In the Right Way ▶ Not in our own _____. (vs. 12–13)

- Upward Focus – "Rejoicing in hope, persevering in tribulation, devoted to prayer."

- Outward Focus – "Contributing to the needs of the saints, practicing (pursuing) hospitality."

- **WHY IS AUTHENTIC COMMUNITY SO IMPORTANT TO JESUS?**

"My prayer is not for them alone. I pray also for those who will believe in me through their message, that all of them may be one, Father, just as you are in me and I am in you. May they also be in us so that the world may believe that you have sent me."

JOHN 17:20-21 (NIV)

Talk It Over

1. Share a time when some friends (authentic community) met a real need in your life that helped you make it through a difficult time. Who do you do that for?

2. What's the biggest barrier that keeps the real you from meeting real needs for the right reasons in the right way?

3. How much does "busyness" impact your ability to see and meet needs? What would it look like for you to slow down?

4. What are some signs or indicators that we are not serving for the right reasons?

5. As a group, brainstorm as many examples as possible when Jesus noticed and met a need.

Live It Out – B.I.O.

Bio is a word that is synonymous with "life." Found in those three simple letters — B.I.O. — is the key to helping you become the person God wants you to be.

B = COME "BEFORE GOD" DAILY

Meet with Him personally through prayer and His word to enjoy His presence, receive His direction, and follow His will.

I = DO LIFE "IN COMMUNITY" WEEKLY

Structure your week to personally connect in safe relationships that provide love, support, transparency, challenge, and accountability.

O = BE "ON MISSION" 24/7

Cultivate a mindset to live out Jesus' love for others through acts of sacrifice as well as service at home, work, play, and church.

Come Before God

6. Read Luke 13:10–17. In this story, what lessons can we learn from Jesus about meeting real needs for the right reason in the right way?

_____

_____

_____

Do Life In Community

7. What does it look like to give "preference to one another in honor"? Be specific.

    _____

    _____

    _____

Be On Mission

8. John 17:20–21 (NIV) says, "My prayer is not for them alone. I pray also for those who will believe in me through their message, that all of them may be one, Father, just as you are in me and I am in you. May they also be in us so that the world may believe that you have sent me."

    What stands out to you from this passage? According to this passage, what is at stake in regards to our community and unity?

    _____

    _____

    _____

Accelerate (20 minutes that turns concepts into convictions)

Inspiration comes from hearing God's Word. **Motivation** grows by discussing God's Word. **Transformation** occurs when you study it for yourself. If you want to "accelerate" your growth, here is an assignment you can do at home each week. Our convictions become even stronger when we dig into Scripture and discover truth for ourselves. To help you get the most out of this exercise, consider partnering with somebody in your group who will also commit to doing the assignment this week. Then, after you have each finished the assignment, agree to spend 10 minutes sharing what you learned and what you are applying.

Come Before God

1. Carefully read this classic story of servanthood from John 13.

¹Before the Passover celebration, Jesus knew that his hour had come to leave this world and return to his Father. He had loved his disciples during his ministry on earth, and now he loved them to the very end. ²It was time for supper, and the devil had already prompted Judas, son of Simon Iscariot, to betray Jesus. ³Jesus knew that the Father had given him authority over everything and that he had come from God and would return to God. ⁴So he got up from the table, took off his robe, wrapped a towel around his waist, ⁵and poured water into a basin. Then he began to wash the disciples' feet, drying them with the towel he had around him.

⁶When Jesus came to Simon Peter, Peter said to him, "Lord, are you going to wash my feet?" ⁷Jesus replied, "You don't understand now what I am doing, but someday you will." ⁸"No," Peter protested, "you will never ever wash my feet!" Jesus replied, "Unless I wash you, you won't belong to me." ⁹Simon Peter exclaimed, "Then wash my hands and head as well, Lord, not just my feet!"

¹⁰Jesus replied, "A person who has bathed all over does not need to wash, except for the feet, to be entirely clean. And you disciples are clean, but not all of you." ¹¹For Jesus knew who would betray him. That is what he meant when he said, "Not all of you are clean."

¹²After washing their feet, he put on his robe again and sat down and asked, "Do you understand what I was doing? ¹³You call me 'Teacher' and 'Lord,' and you are right, because that's what I am. ¹⁴And since I, your Lord and Teacher, have washed your feet, you ought to wash each other's feet. ¹⁵I have given you an example to follow. Do as I have done to you. ¹⁶I tell you the truth, slaves

are not greater than their master. Nor is the messenger more important than the one who sends the message. ¹⁷Now that you know these things, God will bless you for doing them.

JOHN 13:1–17 (NLT)

2. What do you think was the response of the disciples as Jesus went over, grabbed the water basin and towel, and started washing their feet? Do you think they were surprised? Indifferent? Glad? Oblivious?

_____

_____

_____

3. Why do you think Peter said, "you will never wash my feet"? And what do you think Jesus meant when he said, "Unless I wash you, you won't belong to me."?

_____

_____

_____

4. Matthew 20:25–27 (NLT) says, "But Jesus called them together and said, "You know that the rulers in this world lord it over their people, and officials flaunt their authority over those under them. But among you it will be different. Whoever wants to be a leader among you must be your servant, and whoever wants to be first among you must become your slave."

Jesus contrasts the world's view of leadership and the kingdom view of leadership. In the space below, write out 2 lists: one that describes the characters of worldly leadership and another list that describes servant leadership.

The World's Way

1.

2.

3.

4.

5.

The Jesus Way

1.

2.

3.

4.

5.

Do Life In Community

5. Think about the people in your small group or relational network. How could you bless someone by "picking up the towel" and serving them? Now go do it!

    _____

    _____

    _____

Be On Mission

6. According to Romans 12:13, one of the marks of true community is that it has an outward focus. We practice hospitality, which literally means we "pursue strangers." Spend a few moments praying and thinking about someone that you could bless by meeting a need. Now, make a plan for how you will meet that need.

    _____

    _____

    _____

session 11

How To Overcome the Evil Aimed at You

Take It In Watch the video

> You have heard that it was said, 'Love your neighbor and hate your enemy.' But I tell you: Love your enemies and pray for those who persecute you, that you may be sons of your Father in heaven. He causes His sun to rise on the evil and the good, and sends rain on the righteous and the unrighteous. If you love those who love you, what reward will you get? Are not even the tax collectors doing that? And if you greet only your brothers, what are you doing more than others? Do not even pagans do that? Be perfect, therefore, as your heavenly Father is perfect.
>
> **MATTHEW 5:43–48 (NASB)**

It is not hard to be a Romans 12 Christian... it is _____.

A Romans 12 Christian

1.   The commands of Romans 12 are a faith response to Romans chapters 1–11.

2.   Romans 12 Christians focus on _____ not rules or religious activity.

3.   Romans 12 Christians' highest aim is _____.

   - Loving God through a surrendered life. (v.1)

   - Refusing to love the world's false promises. (v.2)

   - Loving ourselves for who God made us to be. (v.3–8)

   - Loving fellow believers through sacrificial service. (v.9–13)

   - Loving our enemies by supernaturally returning good for evil. (v.14–21)

Supernaturally Responding to Evil:

> Bless those who persecute you; bless and do not curse. Rejoice with those who rejoice; mourn with those who mourn. Live in harmony with one another. Do not be proud, but be willing to associate with people of low position. Do not be conceited. Do not repay anyone evil for evil. Be careful to do what is right in the eyes of everybody. If it is possible, as far as it depends on you, live at peace with everyone. Do not take revenge, my friends, but leave room for God's wrath, for it is written: "It is mine to avenge; I will repay," says the Lord.
>
> On the contrary: If your enemy is hungry, feed him; if he is thirsty, give him something to drink. In doing this, you will heap burning coals on his head." Do not be overcome by evil, but overcome evil with good.

ROMANS 12:14–21 (NIV)

A Romans 12 Response to Personal Attack

Positive Command = "_____ those who persecute you"

- Forgiveness - Bless those who persecute you; bless and do not curse

3 Phases of Forgiveness

1. Forgive—it is a _____

2. Forgiving—it is a _____

Forgiving is choosing to give another person what they need the most, when they deserve it the least, at great personal cost.

3. Forgiven—it is _____

   - Identification — "Rejoice with those who rejoice; mourn with those who mourn."

   - Association — "Live in harmony with one another. Do not be proud, but be willing to associate with people of low position. Do not be conceited."

Talk It Over

1. Perhaps today's teaching has brought to the surface a painful situation you are facing right now. Don't be afraid to ask your group for prayer. You don't have to share the details, but you need the prayer and support of Christian friends. Spend whatever time is necessary to pray for those in your group who are dealing with relational wounds.

2. Share about a time when you had to forgive someone who hurt you. How did you come to the place where you could forgive?

   _____

   _____

   _____

3. Have someone read Matthew 18:21–35. At the end of the story, the man who refused to forgive was handed over to be tortured. How is refusing to forgive like handing ourselves over to be tortured?

   _____

   _____

   _____

4. This passage in Romans 12 calls on us to not be proud or conceited. Why is this relevant to a discussion on forgiving those who have hurt us?

   _____

   _____

   _____

Live It Out – B.I.O.

Bio is a word that is synonymous with "life." Found in those three simple letters — B.I.O. — is the key to helping you become the person God wants you to be.

B = COME "BEFORE GOD" DAILY

Meet with Him personally through prayer and His word to enjoy His presence, receive His direction, and follow His will.

I = DO LIFE "IN COMMUNITY" WEEKLY

Structure your week to personally connect in safe relationships that provide love, support, transparency, challenge, and accountability.

O = BE "ON MISSION" 24/7

Cultivate a mindset to live out Jesus' love for others through acts of sacrifice as well as service at home, work, play, and church.

Come Before God

5. Colossians 3:13 (NLT) says, "You must make allowance for each other's faults and forgive the person who offends you. Remember, the Lord forgave you, so you must forgive others."

    What does it mean to "make allowance" for the faults of others?

    _____

    _____

    _____

    How does remembering God's forgiveness help in your journey with forgiveness?

    _____

    _____

    _____

Do Life In Community

6. When you are in the process of forgiving, what can your friends and small group do to help you? What kind of accountability do you need during that time?

    _____

    _____

    _____

Be On Mission

7. Go back and read Matthew 5:43–48. How can forgiving and blessing those who have hurt us be a means of drawing people to Christ?

_____

_____

_____

Accelerate (20 minutes that turns concepts into convictions)

Inspiration comes from hearing God's Word. **Motivation** grows by discussing God's Word. **Transformation** occurs when you study it for yourself. If you want to "accelerate" your growth, here is an assignment you can do at home each week. Our convictions become even stronger when we dig into Scripture and discover truth for ourselves. To help you get the most out of this exercise, consider partnering with somebody in your group who will also commit to doing the assignment this week. Then, after you have each finished the assignment, agree to spend 10 minutes sharing what you learned and what you are applying.

Come Before God

1. Read Matthew 18:21–35 carefully and slowly. Try to emotionally identify with each of the characters in the story.

    26"In your anger do not sin": Do not let the sun go down while you are still angry, 27and do not give the devil a foothold.

    EPHESIANS 4:26–27 (NIV)

    29Do not let any unwholesome talk come out of your mouths, but only what is helpful for building others up according to their needs, that it may benefit those who listen. 30And do not grieve the Holy Spirit of God, with whom you were sealed for the day of redemption. 31Get rid of all bitterness, rage and anger, brawling and slander, along with every form of malice. ³²Be kind and compassionate to one another, forgiving each other, just as in Christ God forgave you.

EPHESIANS 4:29–32 (NIV)

2. Verse 27 warns about giving the devil a foothold in our lives.

    Why is the imagery of a foothold a good analogy for our anger and unwillingness to forgive?

    _____

    _____

    _____

3. In what ways does our anger and unwillingness to forgive give the devil a foothold?

    _____

    _____

    _____

4. From this passage, make a list of things Paul tell us NOT to do, and then make a list of things he tells us TO do.

Don't Do	Do
1. No unwholesome talk	1. Build others up
2.	2.
3.	3.
4.	4.
5.	5.

5. If there is a person you need to forgive, get alone with God this week and make a list of all the specific things this person did to hurt you. Then, go through your list and one by one choose to forgive that person for these hurts. Choose to release rather than re-live your hurts.

Do Life In Community

6. If you are in a situation where you are working through a relational hurt or conflict, ask a friend to help you in this journey. Ask them to pray for you and to keep you accountable for "blessing and not cursing."

Be On Mission

7. There is nothing particularly noble about loving those who love us. Jesus says that even tax collectors do that. This week, go out of your way to love someone in your world that is hard to love. And ask God to give you a heart for loving that person from this point forward.

session 12

How To Overcome the Evil Aimed at You
PART TWO

Positive Command = "Bless those who persecute you" (covered in session 11)

Negative Command = "Don't take your own _____"

> Do not repay anyone evil for evil. Be careful to do what is right in the eyes of everybody. If it is possible, as far as it depends on you, live at peace with everyone. Do not take revenge, my friends, but leave room for God's wrath, for it is written: 'It is mine to avenge; I will repay,' says the Lord. On the contrary: 'If your enemy is hungry, feed him; if he is thirsty, give him something to drink. In doing this, you will heap burning coals on his head.'

ROMANS 12:17–20 (NIV)

- Personal retaliation is a _____ response for God's people.

- Personal retaliation is prohibited because:

   1. It usurps God's role as _____.

   2. It is an ineffective means of bringing about _____.

Supernatural Result = _____ Will Overcome Evil

> Do not be overcome by evil, but overcome evil with good.

ROMANS 12:21 (NIV)

Talk It Over

1. What would happen in your life, your group, your church, and your community if—for the next twelve months—your group chose to become Romans 12 Christians?

   _____

   _____

   _____

2. For you personally, in what way has this Romans 12 series changed your perspective about the Christian life? What impact will this have on how you live?

   _____

   _____

   _____

3. Going forward, what do you need from the people in this group in order to keep the Romans 12 journey alive in your life?

   _____

   _____

   _____

4. Take each of the five areas and write out two statements that you want to characterize your life in those areas.

   _____

   _____

   _____

   This is worth your time and will help crystallize your thinking. Take a few minutes to do this individually. Once you have written these out, spend some time sharing these with your group.

Surrendered to God

Example: God, from this day forward, I am all in.

-

-

Separate from the World's Values

-

-

Sober in Self-Assessment

-

-

Serving in Love

-

-

Supernaturally Overcoming Evil with Good

-

-

Now, let's take a few minutes to jump into this week's lesson on overcoming evil with good.

5. How did Jesus model the concept of overcoming evil with good in His life? In His death?

_____

_____

_____

Live It Out – B.I.O.

Bio is a word that is synonymous with "life." Found in those three simple letters — B.I.O. — is the key to helping you become the person God wants you to be.

B = COME "BEFORE GOD" DAILY

Meet with Him personally through prayer and His word to enjoy His presence, receive His direction, and follow His will.

I = DO LIFE "IN COMMUNITY" WEEKLY

Structure your week to personally connect in safe relationships that provide love, support, transparency, challenge, and accountability.

O = BE "ON MISSION" 24/7

Cultivate a mindset to live out Jesus' love for others through acts of sacrifice as well as service at home, work, play, and church.

Come Before God

6. Read Romans 13:1-5. How does this passage in Romans 12 on forgiveness square with the teaching of Paul in the next chapter about the need for justice in society? Are the two contradictory?

_____

_____

_____

Do Life In Community

7. What are some practical ways that you can "heaping burning coals" on the head of a person who has wounded you?

_____

_____

_____

Be On Mission

8. As a result of this session, is there some step of obedience that you sense God is asking you to take?

_____

_____

_____

Accelerate (20 minutes that turns concepts into convictions)

Inspiration comes from hearing God's Word. **Motivation** grows by discussing God's Word. **Transformation** occurs when you study it for yourself. If you want to "accelerate" your growth, here is an assignment you can do at home each week. Our convictions become even stronger when we dig into Scripture and discover truth for ourselves. To help you get the most out of this exercise, consider partnering with somebody in your group who will also commit to doing the assignment this week. Then, after you have each finished the assignment, agree to spend 10 minutes sharing what you learned and what you are applying.

Come Before God

1. Let's finish this series by going back to Romans 12. Even though we have been in Romans 12 for several weeks, take some time to read through the whole chapter again. Hopefully, you will now read this chapter through a different lens than you did a few weeks ago.

2. Read through Romans 12 a second time, and this time circle the words or phrases that have most impacted you during this series.

3. Now, write down the 3 most significant ways this series has impacted you.

   •

   •

   •

4. As you complete this series, what would you like to say to God? You might want to consider writing out your prayer.

   _____

   _____

   _____

Do Life In Community

5. Get together this coming week with someone that went through this series with you. Spend some time discussing the following question: What are some ways we can keep the Romans 12 journey alive, and how can we help each other in that journey?

   _____

   _____

   _____

Be On Mission

6. If you are going to actually live as a Romans 12 Christian, what is the most radical change you need to make? What step of obedience do you need to take to make that change?

    _____

    _____

    _____

Small Group Leader Resources

Group Agreement

People come to groups with a variety of expectations. The purpose of a group agreement is simply to make sure everyone is on the same page and that we have some common expectations.

The following Group Agreement is a tool to help you discuss specific guidelines during your first meeting. Modify anything that does not work for your group, then be sure to discuss the questions in the section called Our Game Plan. This will help you to have an even greater group experience.

WE AGREE TO THE FOLLOWING PRIORITIES

- **Take the Bible Seriously** — To seek to understand and apply God's truth in the Bible.

- **Group Attendance** — To give priority to the group meeting. I will call if I am going to be absent or late.

- **Safe Environment** — To create a safe place where people can be heard and feel loved. There are no snap judgments or simple fixes.

- **Respectful Discussion** — To speak in a respectful and honoring way to others in the group.

- **Be Confidential** — To keep anything that is shared strictly confidential and within the group.

- **Spiritual Health** — To give group members permission to help me live a godly, healthy spiritual life that is pleasing to God.

- **Building Relationships** — To get to know the other members of the group and pray for them regularly.

- **Pursue B.I.O.** — To encourage and challenge each other in coming "before God" daily, doing life together "in community", and being "on mission" 24/7.

- **Prayer** — To regularly pray with and for each other.

- **Other**

  _____

  _____

Our Game Plan

1. What day and time will we meet?

    _____

    _____

    _____

2. Where will we meet?

    _____

    _____

    _____

3. How long will we meet each week?

    _____

    _____

    _____

4. What will we do for refreshments?

    _____

    _____

    _____

5. What will we do about childcare?

    _____

    _____

    _____

How to Make This a Meaningful Experience for Your Group

BEFORE THE GROUP ARRIVES

1. **Be prepared.** Your personal preparation can make a huge difference in the quality of the group experience. We strongly suggest previewing both the DVD teaching by Chip Ingram and the Study Guide.

2. **Pray for your group members by name.** Ask God to use your time together to touch the heart of every person in your group. Expect God to challenge and change people as a result of this study.

3. **Provide refreshments.** There's nothing like food to help a group relax and connect with each other. For the first week, we suggest you prepare a snack. After that, ask other group members to bring the food so that they share in the responsibilities of the group and make a commitment to return.

4. **Relax.** Don't try to imitate someone else's style of leading a group. Lead the group in a way that fits your style and temperament. Remember that people may feel nervous showing up for a small group study, so put them at ease when they arrive. Make sure to have all the details covered prior to your group meeting, so that once people start arriving, you can focus on them.

Group Meeting Format

TAKE IT IN (WATCH THE VIDEO)

1. **Get the video ready.** Each video session will have three components. First, Chip will spend a few minutes introducing this week's topic. Next, you will watch the content that Chip taught in front of a live audience—this portion of the video will be roughly 20-25 minutes in length. Lastly, Chip will share some closing thoughts and set up the discussion time for your group.

2. **Have ample materials.** Before you start the video, make sure everyone has their own copy of the study guide. Encourage the group to open to this week's session and follow along with the teaching. There is an outline in the study guide with an opportunity to fill in the outline.

3. **Arrange the room.** Set up the chairs in the room so that everyone can see the television. Arrange the room in such a way that it is conducive to discussion.

TALK IT OVER

Here are some guidelines for leading the discussion time:

1. **Make this a discussion, not a lecture.** Resist the temptation to do all the talking and to answer your own questions. Don't be afraid of a few moments of silence while people formulate their responses.

   Don't feel like you need to have all the answers. There is nothing wrong with simply saying, "I don't know the answer to that, but I'll see if I can find an answer this week."

2. **Encourage everyone to participate.** Don't let one person dominate, but also don't pressure quieter members to speak. Be patient. Ask good follow-up questions, and be sensitive to delicate issues.

3. **Affirm people's participation and input.** If an answer is clearly wrong, ask "What led you to that conclusion?" or ask what the rest of the group thinks. If a disagreement arises, don't be too quick to shut it down. The discussion can draw out important perspectives. If you still can't resolve a disagreement, offer to research it further and return to the issue next week.

   However, if someone goes on the offensive and engages in personal attacks, you will need to step in as the leader. In the midst of spirited discussion, we must also remember that people are fragile and there is no place for disrespect.

4. **Detour when necessary.** If an important question is raised that is not in the study guide, take time to discuss it. Also, if someone shares something personal and emotional, take time for them. Stop and pray for them right then. Allow the Holy Spirit room to maneuver, and follow His prompting when the discussion changes direction.

5. **Subgroup.** One of the principles of small group life is "when numbers go up, sharing goes down." If you have a large group, sometimes you may want to split up into groups of 4-6 people for the discussion time. This

is a great way to give everyone, even the quieter members, a chance to share. Choose someone in the group to guide each of the smaller groups through the discussion. This involves others in the leadership of the group and provides an opportunity for training new leaders.

6. **Pray.** Be sensitive to the fact that some people in your group may be uncomfortable praying out loud. As a general rule, don't call on people to pray unless you have asked them ahead of time or have heard them pray in public. But this can also be a time to help people build their confidence to pray in a group. Consider having prayer times that ask people to just say a word or sentence of thanks to God.

LIVE IT OUT – B.I.O.

Bio is a word that is synonymous with "life." Found in those three simple letters — B.I.O. — is the key to helping you become the person God wants you to be.

B = COME "BEFORE GOD" DAILY

Meet with Him personally through prayer and His word to enjoy His presence, receive His direction, and follow His will.

I = DO LIFE "IN COMMUNITY" WEEKLY

Structure your week to personally connect in safe relationships that provide love, support, transparency, challenge, and accountability.

O = BE "ON MISSION" 24/7

Cultivate a mindset to live out Jesus' love for others through acts of sacrifice as well as service at home, work, play, and church.

ACCELERATE (20 MINUTES THAT TURNS CONCEPTS INTO CONVICTIONS)

Inspiration comes from hearing God's Word. **Motivation** grows by discussing God's Word. **Transformation** occurs when you study it for yourself. If you want to "accelerate" your growth, here is an assignment you can do at home each week. Our convictions become even stronger when we dig into Scripture and discover truth for ourselves. To help you get the most out of this exercise, consider partnering with somebody in your group who will also commit to do the assignment this week. Then, after you have each finished the assignment, agree to spend 10 minutes sharing what you learned and what you are applying.

Session Notes

Thanks for hosting this series on *True Spirituality*. This compelling series will equip you with a biblical view of discipleship and help you know how to live as a follower of Jesus. Whether you are brand new at leading a small group or you are a seasoned veteran, God is going to use you. God has a long history of using ordinary people to get his work done.

These brief notes are intended to help prepare you for each week's session. By spending just a few minutes each week previewing the video and going over these session notes, you will set the table for a great group experience. Also, don't forget to pray for your group each week.

SESSION 1 — GOD'S DREAM FOR YOUR LIFE

- If your group doesn't know each other well, be sure that you spend some time getting acquainted. Don't rush right into the video lesson. Remember, small groups are not just about a study or a meeting; they are about relationships.

- Be sure to capture everyone's contact information. It is a good idea to send out an email with everybody's contact information so that the group can stay in touch. At the back of your study guide is a roster where people can fill in the names and contact information of the other group members.

- When you are ready to start the session, be sure that each person in your group has a copy of the study guide. The small group study guide is important for people to follow along and to take notes.

- Spend a little time in this first session talking about B.I.O. These three core practices are the pathway to maturity. You will see these letters and terms throughout this curriculum. Start getting your group comfortable with the concepts of "coming before God" daily, "doing life together in community" weekly, and "being on mission" 24/7.

- Lead by example. Sometimes Chip will ask you as the facilitator to lead the way by answering the first question. This allows you to lead by example. Your willingness to share openly about your life will help others feel the permission to do the same.

- Before you wrap up your group time, be sure to introduce the Accelerate exercise in the study guide. This is an assignment everyone can do during the week that will help turbo charge their growth. Encourage them to find a partner in the group whom they can talk to each week about the accelerate exercise.

- It would be a good idea to review the discussion questions for this week's session. In most weeks, there are seven discussion questions. If that is too many for your group to get through, you might want to decide ahead of time which questions you want your group to discuss.

- In Sessions 1 and 2, Chip will do an overview of the five key relationships of a Romans 12 Christian. During Session 1, Chip will cover being "Surrendered to God" and "Separate from the World's Values." It will be helpful for you to memorize these phrases because you will come back to them again and again in this series.

SESSION 2 — GOD'S DREAM FOR YOUR LIFE (PART 2)

- Why not begin your preparation by praying right now for the people in your group. You might even want to keep their names in your Bible. You may also want to ask people in your group how you can pray for them specifically.

- If somebody doesn't come back this week, be sure and follow up with them. Even if you knew they were going to miss the meeting, give them a call or send them an email letting them know that they were missed. It would also be appropriate to have a couple of other people in the group let them know they were missed.

- If you haven't already previewed the video, take the time to do so. It will help you know how to best facilitate the group and which are the best discussion questions for your group.

- This week in question two, you will be asked to read a passage of scripture from Matthew 23. The passage is not printed in your study guide. You will need to have at least one Bible so you can read the passage.

- Question six asks when you have experienced true community. It would be good to think about this ahead of time so you can be the first to answer this question if needed.

SESSION 3 — HOW TO GIVE GOD WHAT HE WANTS THE MOST

- Did anybody miss last week's session? If so, make it a priority to follow up and let them know they were missed. It just might be your care for them that keeps them connected to the group.

- Share the load. One of the ways to raise the sense of ownership within the group is to get them involved in more than just coming to the meeting. Get someone to help with refreshments. Find somebody else to be in charge of the prayer requests. Get someone else to be in charge of any social gathering you plan. Let someone else lead the discussion one night. Give away as much of the responsibility as possible—that's good leadership.

- Think about last week's meeting for a moment. Was there anyone that didn't talk or participate? In every group, there are extroverts and there are introverts. There are people who like to talk and those who are content NOT to talk. Not everyone engages in the same way or at the same level, but you do want to try and create an environment where everyone is welcomed to participate.

- Follow up with your group to see how they did with this week's Accelerate assignment. Don't shame or embarrass anyone who didn't get to the assignment, but honestly challenge them to make this a priority in the coming week.

- This week's session will explore the topic of being surrendered to God. This truth is foundational to the rest of the journey in becoming a Romans 12 Christian. People will be asked to share their fears and challenges in surrendering to God. Help people in your group to know that we all struggle with this, and that this group is a safe place to share honestly.

SESSION 4 — HOW TO GIVE GOD WHAT HE WANTS THE MOST (PART 2)

- Don't feel any pressure to get through all the questions. As people open up and talk, don't move on too quickly. Give them the space to share what is going on inside them.

- Don't be afraid of silence. When you ask people a question, give them time to think about it. Don't feel like you have to fill every quiet moment with words.

- One of the questions this week is about how surrender in the Christian life is like marriage. Give this question some thought and write down a short list of ways that surrender to God is like marriage. Then, only share those on your list that don't come up in the group discussion.

- This week in the "in community" question, people in your group will be asked how others in the group can support them in the journey to live a surrendered life. This is an important question because it begins getting people involved with each other outside the group meeting.

SESSION 5 — HOW TO GET GOD'S BEST FOR YOUR LIFE

- Confidentiality is crucial to group life. The moment trust is breached, people will shut down and close up. You may want to reiterate the importance of confidentiality this week, just to keep it on people's radar.

- Each time your group meets, take a few minutes to update everyone on what has happened since the last group meeting. Ask people what they are learning and putting into practice. Remember, being a disciple of Jesus means becoming a "doer of the word."

- As you begin this week's session, it would be a good idea to check in with the group regarding the Accelerate exercise that they have been challenged to do as homework. If people are doing the exercise, ask them what they have been learning and how it has been impacting them. If they haven't been doing the exercise, encourage them to commit to it this next week.

- As you talk about being separate from the world's values this week, your group will be asked, "What are some prominent values in our generation that are contrary to God's values?" This should spark some good discussion, but don't let it turn into a political debate or a discussion on everything that's wrong with America.

- The last question this week will ask how we can protect our families from being infected by the world's values. Encourage people to share practical and specific ideas that they use in their own families.

SESSION 6 — HOW TO GET GOD'S BEST FOR YOUR LIFE (PART 2)

- You are now at the halfway point of this series. How is it going? How well is the group connecting? What has been going well and what needs a little work? Are there any adjustments you need to make?

- One way to deepen the level of community within your group is to spend time together outside the group meeting. If you haven't already done so, plan something that will allow you to get to know each other better. Also, consider having someone else in the group take responsibility for a fellowship event.

- In this session, Chip will introduce a Bible Study method referred to as 2PROAPT. Spend some time going over this tool and encourage people to give it a try this next week.

- This week, you will be asked to share a verse or passage of scripture that has been especially meaningful in your life. Be prepared to share first so that others in the group have time to think of a verse or find it in their Bible.

SESSION 7 — HOW TO COME TO GRIPS WITH THE REAL YOU

- Consider sending an email to each person in your group this week letting them know you prayed for them today. Also, let them know that you're grateful that they're in the group.

- Take a few minutes this week before you get into the study to talk about the impact of this series so far. Ask people what they are learning, applying, and changing in their lives. For this series to have lasting impact, it has to be more than just absorbing information. Challenge your group to put what they are learning into action.

- Revisit the importance of B.I.O. this week. Reinforce the importance of people integrating these core practices in their lives. For example, talk about the priority of coming before God each day and submitting to the authority of God's truth.

- The opening question this week will ask your group what messages they got from their parents that shaped their view of themselves. This should be a very insightful discussion, but don't let someone use this as an opportunity to dominate and share their whole family upbringing. Keep the discussion moving.

- Also, you will be asked as a group to brainstorm a list of statements that are true about your identity in Christ. To get started, look at Romans 8 and Ephesians 1:3-14. It would be a good idea for you to look at these passages ahead of time. Write down a few thoughts that might help jumpstart the discussion.

SESSION 8 — HOW TO COME TO GRIPS WITH THE REAL YOU (PART 2)

- The only thing better than good questions are good follow-up questions. Follow-up questions are like onions—each one allows another layer to be peeled back and get beneath the surface.

- In your group meetings, be sure to take adequate time for prayer. Don't just tack it on at the end of the meeting simply out of obligation. Also, don't be afraid to stop the meeting and pray for someone who shares a need or a struggle.

- This session should be a lot of fun and should be very encouraging to the group. Some of the discussion time will be spent exploring people's gifts and talents as well as brainstorming how God might use them.

- During the discussion time this week, your group will be asked to encourage and affirm one another. It's probably best for you to wait until the end to share. That way if someone has been left out, you can share affirmation of them.

- At the end of your discussion time, your group will be asked to consider doing a project that would use the gifts and talents of those in the group. Take this challenge seriously. Don't feel as though you have to do all the work for this project. Find someone in the group who has the time and passion for your project and let them be the point person.

SESSION 9 — HOW TO EXPERIENCE AUTHENTIC COMMUNITY

- This week (or next) might be a good week to give someone else a chance to facilitate. Right now, think of someone in your group that you believe could facilitate. Give them enough advance notice to prepare, but give them a call. It's a great way for them to develop their own leadership skills.

- Sometime during the session this week, follow up on your plans to do a group project. Have you identified a project? Set a date? Named a point person? Solidify your plans and try to get everyone in the group to participate. Serving together deepens the bonds of relationship.

- Your group has now been together for nine sessions. This is a great time to talk about going deeper in community as a group. And that is exactly what Chip is going to talk about this week. One of the keys to deepening community is to spend time together outside the group. Encourage people to get together with others in the group apart from the group meeting.

SESSION 10 — HOW TO EXPERIENCE AUTHENTIC COMMUNITY (PART 2)

- Don't forget to celebrate what God has been teaching you and doing in the lives of group members. You might want to take some time at the beginning of this week's session to have people share how this series has impacted them.

- As you are nearing the end of this curriculum, it's a good time to start thinking about what your group will do after this series is over. You can find several other small group curriculums by Chip Ingram at LivingontheEdge.org.

- During this week's session, you will talk about one of the biggest barriers to authentic community: busyness. Have an honest discussion about the impact of busyness. Challenge people to get serious about slowing down their lives and making more time for relationships. Get practical and specific.

- Also this week, your group will be asked to brainstorm as many examples as possible when Jesus "noticed" and met a need. You might want to get out your Bible ahead of time, and scan through the gospels making a short list of places where Jesus noticed and met a need.

SESSION 11 — HOW TO OVERCOME THE EVIL AIMED AT YOU

- After this session, there will only be one more week in the study. Be sure that everyone is clear about what your group is doing after this study.

- As this series winds down, this is a good time to plan some kind of party or fellowship for when you complete the study. Find the "party person" in your group, and ask them to take on the responsibility of planning a fun experience for the group. Also, use this party as a time for people to share how God has used this series to grow them and change them.

- This week's session will focus on overcoming the evil that has been aimed at us. It is likely that this teaching will bring to the surface a painful situation that some in your group are facing right now. If that is true, don't be afraid to stop and take time to pray for those in the group who are struggling to forgive someone. They don't have to share the details, but they need the prayer and support of Christian friends. Spend whatever time is necessary to pray for those in your group who are dealing with relational wounds.

- Also, the group will be asked to share about a time when they had to forgive someone. This might be a time when you can lead the way by sharing from your own life.

SESSION 12 — HOW TO OVERCOME THE EVIL AIMED AT YOU (PART 2)

- Congratulations! You have made it to the last week. Facilitating a session on difficult issues is no small task. Thanks for your leadership and willingness to shepherd your group through this series.

- The discussion for this session will break down into 2 segments. First, your group will be asked to discuss how they can keep the Romans 12 journey alive after the group study. As part of this discussion, each person will be asked to take each of the five areas and write out two statements that they want to characterize their life in that area. This is worth your time and will help the group crystallize their thinking. Take a few minutes to do this individually.

  Then, once you have written these out, spend some time having the group share their statements with each other.

- You will conclude the discussion time by talking specifically about this week's lesson on overcoming the evil aimed at you.

Prayer and Praise

One of the most important things you can do in your group is to pray with and for each other. Write down each other's concerns here so you can remember to pray for these requests during the week.

Use the Follow Up box to record an answer to prayer or to write down how you might want to follow up with the person making the request. This could be a phone call, an email, or a card. Your personal concern will mean a lot!

DATE	PERSON	PRAYER REQUEST	FOLLOW UP

DATE	PERSON	PRAYER REQUEST	FOLLOW UP

DATE	PERSON	PRAYER REQUEST	FOLLOW UP

DATE	PERSON	PRAYER REQUEST	FOLLOW UP

DATE	PERSON	PRAYER REQUEST	FOLLOW UP

DATE	PERSON	PRAYER REQUEST	FOLLOW UP

What's Next?

More Group Studies from Chip Ingram:

Balancing Life's Demands
Biblical Priorities for a Busy Life
Busy, tired and stressed out? Learn how to put "first things first" and find peace in the midst of pressure and adversity.

Culture Shock
A Biblical Response to Today's Most Divisive Issues
Bring light—not heat—to divisive issues, such as abortion, homosexuality, sex, politics, the environment, and more.

Doing Good
What Happens When Christians Really Live Like Christians
This series clarifies what Doing Good will do in you and then through you, for the benefit of others and the glory of God.

Experiencing God's Dream for Your Marriage
Practical Tools for a Thriving Marriage
Examine God's design for marriage and the real life tools and practices that will transform it for a lifetime.

Five Lies that Ruin Relationships
Building Truth-Based Relationships
Uncover five powerful lies that wreck relationships and experience the freedom of understanding how to recognize God's truth.

The Genius of Generosity
Lessons from a Secret Pact Between Friends
The smartest financial move you can make is to invest in God's Kingdom. Learn His design for wise giving and generous living.

The Real God
How He Longs for You to See Him
A deeper look at seven attributes of God's character that will change the way you think, pray and live.

Good to Great in God's Eyes
10 Practices Great Christians Have in Common
If you long for spiritual breakthrough, take a closer look at ten powerful practices that will rekindle a fresh infusion of faith.

The Real Heaven
What the Bible Actually Says
Chip Ingram digs into scripture to reveal what heaven will be like, what we'll do there, and how we're to prepare for eternity today.

Holy Ambition
Turning God-Shaped Dreams Into Reality
Do you long to turn a God-inspired dream into reality? Learn how God uses everyday believers to accomplish extraordinary things.

House or Home: Marriage Edition
God's Blueprint for a Great Marriage
Get back to the blueprint and examine God's plan for marriages that last for a lifetime.

House or Home: Parenting Edition
God's Blueprint for Biblical Parenting
Timeless truths about God's blueprint for parenting, and the potential to forever change the trajectory of your family.

The Invisible War
The Believer's Guide to Satan, Demons and Spiritual Warfare
Learn how to clothe yourself with God's "spiritual armor" and be confident of victory over the enemy of your soul.

Love, Sex and Lasting Relationships **UPDATED**
God's Prescription to Enhance Your Love Life
Do you believe in "true love"? Discover a better way to find love, stay in love, and build intimacy that lasts a lifetime.

Overcoming Emotions that Destroy
Constructive Tools for Destructive Emotions
We all struggle with destructive emotions that can ruin relationships. Learn God's plan to overcome angry feelings for good.

Spiritual Simplicity
Doing Less · Loving More
If you crave simplicity and yearn for peace this study is for you. Spiritual simplicity can only occur when we do less and love more.

Transformed
The Miracle of Life Change
Ready to make a change? Explore God's process of true transformation and learn to spot barriers that hold you back from receiving God's best.

True Spirituality
Becoming a Romans 12 Christian
We live in a world that is activity-heavy and relationship-light. Learn the next steps toward True Spirituality.

Why I Believe
Answers to Life's Most Difficult Questions
Can miracles be explained? Is there really a God? There are solid, logical answers about claims of the Christian faith.

Your Divine Design
Discover, Develop and Deploy Your Spiritual Gifts
How has God uniquely wired you? Discover God's purpose for spiritual gifts and how to identify your own.

Download the Chip Ingram App

The Chip Ingram App delivers daily devotionals, broadcasts, message notes, blog articles and more right on your mobile device.